Complete Course of Chess

Aryan Jain Ascanio

AuthorHouse™ UK
1663 Liberty Drive
Bloomington, IN 47403 USA
www.authorhouse.co.uk
UK TFN: 0800 0148641 (Toll Free inside the UK)
UK Local: 02036 956322 (+44 20 3695 6322 from outside the UK)

Editor: Aryan Jain Ascanio
Interior Design: Aryan Jain Ascanio
Cover Design: Aryan Jain Ascanio

This book is printed on acid-free paper.

ISBN: 978-1-7283-7587-8 (sc)
ISBN: 978-1-7283-7588-5 (e)

Print information available on the last page.

Published by AuthorHouse 10/31/2022

authorHOUSE®

Contents

Contents

Introduction

Nowadays—due to new technologies like supercomputers—chess is becoming more sophisticated. It can even get boring, since the moment you make a mistake, you can lose the game. This can demotivate some.

However, with this book, I am going to teach you everything you need to know to be at least a level of 1,000 ELO (which is quite high). Chess is a very complex game, so it would be an impossible task to teach all the concepts—all the openings, tactics, and endings—in a single book. Each one could fill a book.

What I will do in this book, then, is teach you all the principles and openings that have helped me win games and tournaments. These will both help you flourish as a player and serve as inspiration. Without further delay, let's get started.

Chapter 1
Tactics

Double attack

A double attack is performed by a piece that attacks two pieces. This allows you to win material. It could be with a check—for example, an attack by a knight that gives a check and at the same time attacks a rook, as in the following position.

Or it can be without a check between two pieces—for instance, a queen and a rook.

X-ray

X-ray refers to the tactic that is performed when a piece that attacks in a straight line or diagonal gives a check to the king, and when the king steps aside, the attacking piece captures the piece that is behind. In other words, the attacking piece eats the piece that is behind the king. This position is an example of such a tactic, where it's black to move.

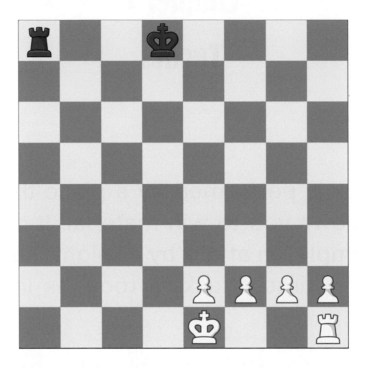

Here a check is delivered, and when the king moves, you capture the rook.

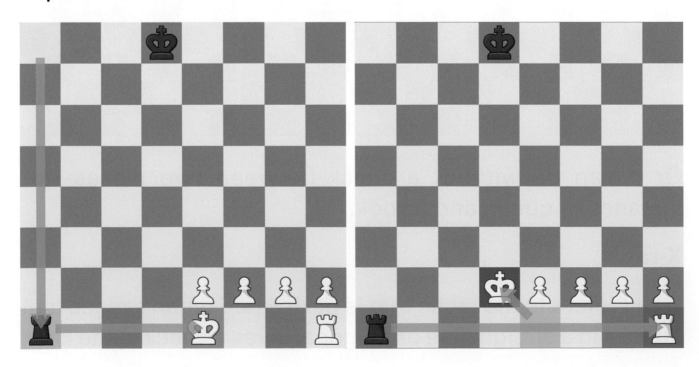

Pin

This is a concept in which a piece is attacked, but it cannot be moved—because if it moves, the king is captured. This is also called *absolute pin*. There is also what is called a *relative pin*, which is the same concept only that in this case, instead of being pinned because of the king's position, it happens because of another piece.

This can be exploited as follows.

We have this position where it is up for white to play, and we can see that the black knight cannot move because otherwise, the white rook would capture the king. So, we as white can attack it. Since it is not able to move, we will win the piece. As follows:

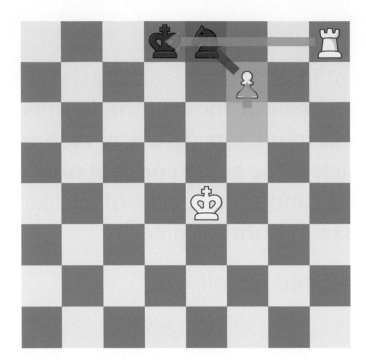

So, in the next move, no matter what black moves, we will have won a knight.

Discovered attack

This tactic is performed when our piece is in the same column or row as the enemy's king, which is not being attacked for the moment because there is a piece of ours in the middle, blocking that action. A discovered attack takes advantage of that; when the piece blocking the check moves, this threatens another piece, while checking the king. This gives the side performing this attack a material advantage.

For example, let's take a famous position from the Petrov opening.

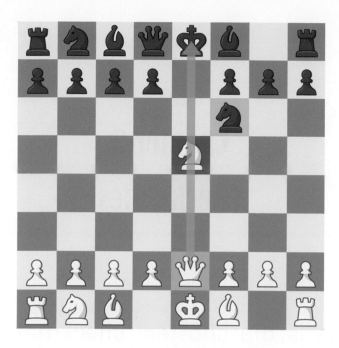

In this position, our queen cannot attack the enemy king because our knight is in the way. If we move the knight anywhere, the king will have to cover himself or move and will not have time to defend whatever we are attacking with the knight. It would be best for our knight to attack the queen while delivering this discovered check, as shown.

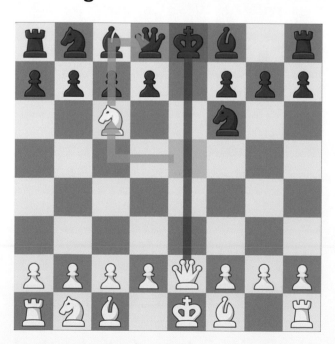

And in this way, we will get a material advantage.

Chapter 2
Checkmates

Fool's mate

The fool's mate is the shortest checkmate that exists in chess. It does not appear much, since the rival has to play somewhat unusual and meaningless moves to bring it about. But I will teach it, since maybe you'll have the chance to perform it.

The mate begins when white makes the f4 move.

Black, following the principles of chess that dictate that the centre must be controlled, makes the e6 move.

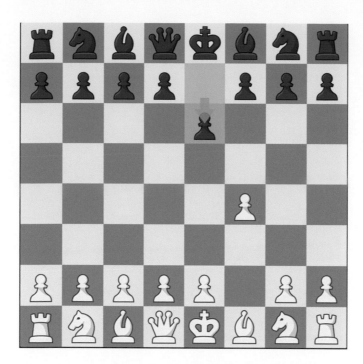

White plays g4.

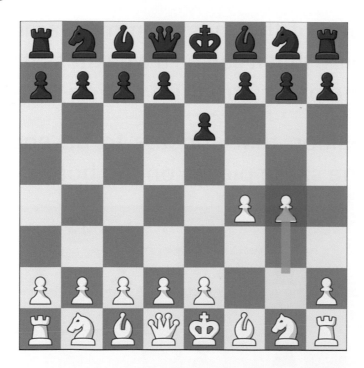

And black performs the fool's mate with the move *queen to h4* (Qh4#, where # indicates checkmate).

Back rank mate

This mate is one of the most common among beginners, who do not realize that it can be a weakness if the king cannot move due to the pawn structure arising when castling.

We have a position that appears to be equal, since both players have the same pieces on the board.

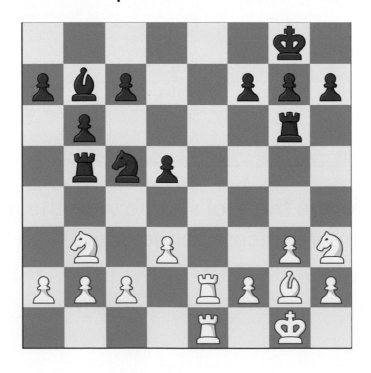

However, white realizes that the enemy king, if attacked across the back rank, has nowhere to go. That is why white makes the move *rook e8 with check*, as the king cannot go anywhere and is not able to cover the check with any other piece. It is checkmate.

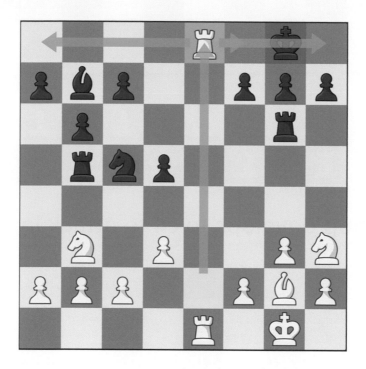

Scholar's mate

This is a mate that all beginners of the game have tried to do once. It is not played at high levels, since a failed attempt at this checkmate can have disastrous consequences. However, I will show it to you to try to get some other victory.

The game would start with both king pawns advanced (e4, e5).

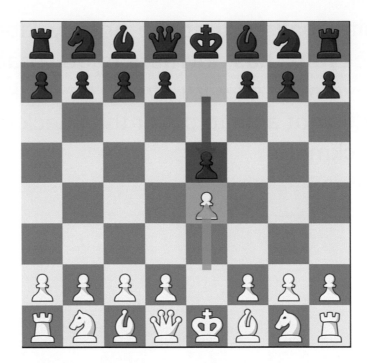

Then, the bishop develops to c4 to attack in f7.

The black pieces develop their knight.

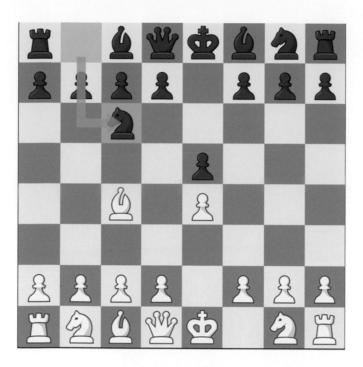

White again attacks the f7 square, with the queen in f3.

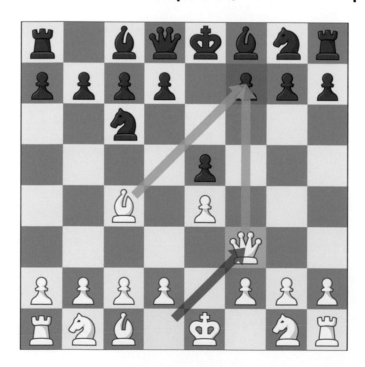

Black, oblivious to everything that has happened, makes any move that does not defend f7.

White checkmates with the queen in f7.

Arabian mate

This mate is given with the knight and a rook. For this to happen, the king has to be in a corner. The knight must be two squares diagonally from the king, with the rook prepared.

We have the king cut to only one column/row by the rook, so that it can only move around the rook; sooner or later, it places itself in the corner. We must have the knight ready in that position when it happens.

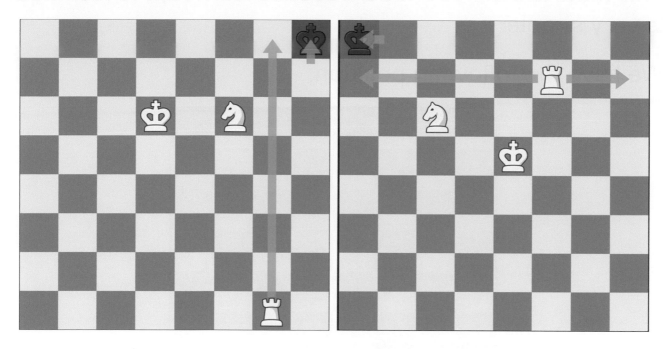

We checkmate with the rook, putting it in front of the king, since the knight protects it and covers other squares where the king might run.

How to checkmate with the pieces

Rook

This mate is a bit laborious, but once learned, the technique is very simple.

We have the following position.

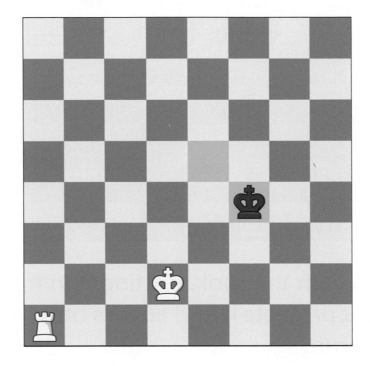

What must be done in this position first is to cut any rows the king might have so that at the end of the sequence, we corner the king against one side of the board. The move *rook to a3* is made so that it cuts row number 3, meaning the king can only be between rows 4 and 8.

In case the king moves back one row, we cut another row so that the king can only be between rows 5 and 8.

If the king has not gone back but rather to one side (in this case, in e4), we must waste a move, since our goal is that our king acts as a knight attacking the rival king. As the king was already placed in this position, we waste some time with the rook.

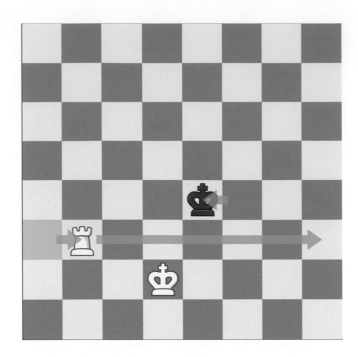

The purpose of this is that the rival king is the one that is cornered. If the enemy king is placed directly in front of our king, we will give it a check with the rook. The king controls all the squares that the rival king would use to move forward, and the rook cuts an entire row. This forces the enemy king to go one row further back and only be able to move from rows 5 to 8.

If the king attacks our rook, the only thing we can do is move the rook from one side of the board to the other in the same row. We only move the row rook when the rival king stands right in front of ours.

From here, the process is always the same: what you have to do is chase the enemy king with your king as if it were a knight giving checks.

This forces the king to stand in front of us sooner or later, or move backward, losing another row in which it can move.

This process will be repeated many times until the final checkmate position, which is as shown.

Two rooks

The checkmate with two rooks is somewhat easier, since after all there are two rooks instead of one, but you have to know the correct technique.

To begin with, place the rooks in the configuration shown.

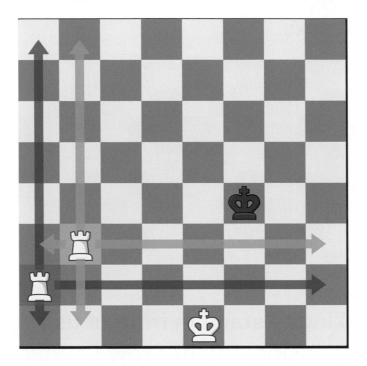

They should not be in the same column or the same row. If they are in the same column or row, they will interfere with each other.

What will be done is to make a series of checks to corner the king against the last row. In this case, it is not necessary to move our king at all.

Always check with the rook that is in the row below, since otherwise the king will be between two rows, and we do not want this.

We want this.

This is with the purpose that the king goes backwards.

In case the king does not attack the rooks, the checkmate will simply be to check all the time with the rooks. Remember that the check you have to give is always with the rook that is below. When you give a check with this rook, on the next move, the rook that you haven't moved before is now the rook that is below.

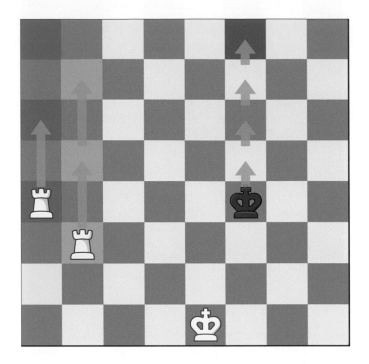

In case the king does attack the rooks at some point, all you have to do is move the rooks from one side of the board to the other (the king is not as fast as the rooks when moving from one side to the other) and continue with the process.

The final position of the checkmate is as shown.

Queen

The mate of the queen is one of the easiest there is, since you simply have to copy what the rival does with their king, as the king cannot attack our queen.

What you have to do is practically be his shadow. If the king moves one square to the right, so does the queen. The king moves a step up, and so does the queen. You copy what the king does until it possesses only two rows through which to move.

As you will observe, as you do this, the king will be trapping himself all the time. If we continue the previous position, the result would be this.

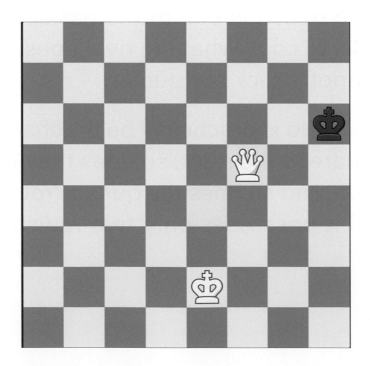

Now what you have to do is make the rival king only have a row or column to move through. The method would be the same as before (keep copying everything the king does) and the result, for example, would be this.

Now all that should be done is to bring our king to where the rival king is, while the rival king is locked up.

And to checkmate, what you have to do is place the queen right in front of the enemy king (it has to be protected by your king, otherwise it is a sacrifice), so the result would be as follows.

Tip: Be very careful when you have to make the enemy king only have one row or column to move in. Make sure it has two squares to move through while you bring your king, because otherwise, it would be a draw for stalemate. Do this until the king only has two squares left, and then bring your king.

Chapter 3
Openings

All good chess players must have a repertoire of openings that adapt to their way of playing. This is something you will choose before playing that suits your particular style. An opening, after all, has two purposes:

1. At the end of the opening, you are in an advantageous position, in case your rival does not know it.
2. If your opponent does know it and plays it perfectly (which is not very common), you will still be in the type of position that you like to play.

Since there are two types of positions—open and closed—each opening has its ideas and its game mode. In this book, I will guide you through openings that have led me to many victories in tournaments. These are easy to play, do not require great memory, and can still be played even among grandmasters at the highest level.

Openings with white

Italian opening

The Italian opening starts with e4. The king's pawn takes two steps. Below is a diagram representing the final position when the opening is finished.

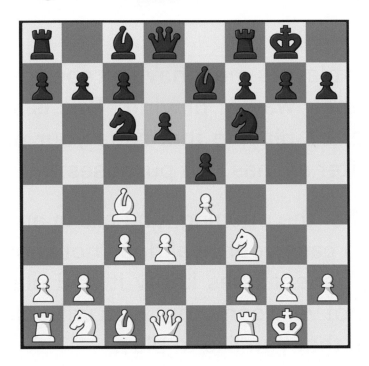

The purpose of this move is to take control of the central squares. They are the most important squares on the board, since almost all the action occurs through these squares.

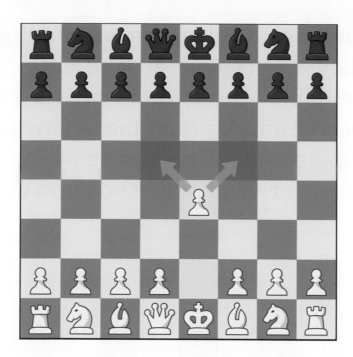

Then black makes the e5 move with the same purpose: to control the central squares and prevent the white pawn from advancing further and taking more squares from the opponent (in this case, the player with the black pieces).

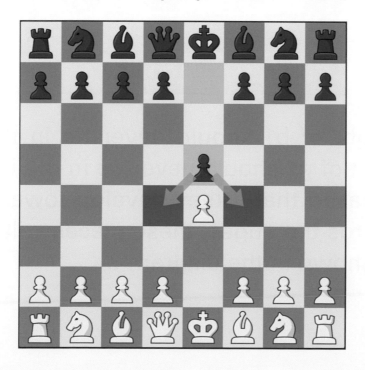

The next thing that the white pieces will do is develop the knight that is in g1 to f3. This move is denoted as Nf3, and it has three purposes: to clear the way so that the king can castle as quickly as possible and be safe; to bring more pieces into the game and be more active (in other words, develop that piece); and to attack the enemy pawn and force the opponent to defend it. This forces the opponent to play the opening we want—and play a position they will not like at all.

Tip: The knight of b1 should never be in the a3 square, and the knight of g1 should never be in the h3 square—for the simple reason that if they develop towards the centre and not towards the edges, these pieces will control more squares. As shown in the diagram …

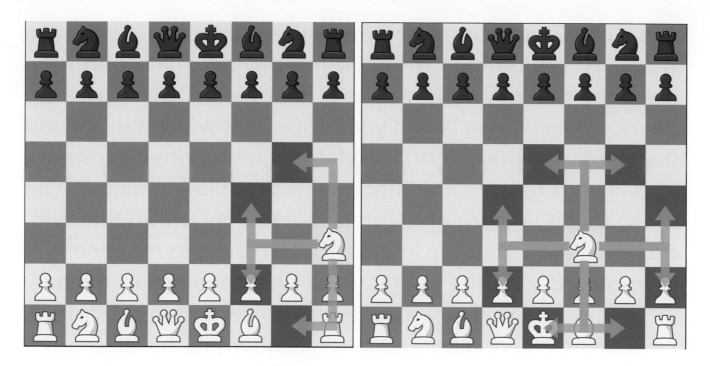

... if the knight develops at the centre, it controls more squares.

Continuing with the opening—once the knight is moved, what black must do is defend the pawn, or it will have a material disadvantage. Black has three possible moves to defend the pawn: with the bishop, with another pawn, or with the knight.

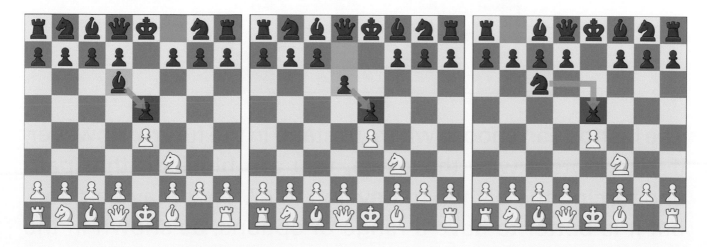

Only defending it with the knight is a correct move, since if you defend yourself with the bishop, you are blocking your pawn of d7, and then further in the game, you will have to spend two tempos to move the bishop again and then move the pawn, which means it is not effective. However, the most likely thing is that your opponent will either defend the pawn with the knight or with the pawn. Both options are correct, but in my experience with the black pieces, I can affirm that it is more uncomfortable to play protecting with the pawn than with the knight, for two simple reasons: if it is protected with the knight, it will be developing a piece, and it leaves a freeway for the bishop so that in the future, it develops wherever you want, as shown in the diagram.

The bishop can choose where to stand in the future. However, if you protect with the pawn, you are blocking that path and forcing the bishop to develop to e7. That may be good, but it is better to have a range of options, as shown in the diagram.

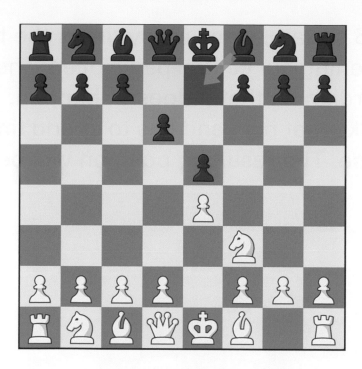

Here, the pawn blocks the bishop's path. If you want to take out the bishop to another place in the future, you will have to wait until the pawn can be moved again so that it doesn't get in the way, which does not usually happen and which the white pieces do not allow.

The other advantage of protecting with the knight would be that in the future, the pawn of d7 will be able to choose whether to advance one or two squares. This depends on the position. The other way forces the pawn to be in d6 for a long time, most likely.

Both moves are played at lower levels, but protecting with d6 has a higher defeat rate and is also played a little less than knight development.

Once black develops their knight, what will be done is to develop the bishop from f1 to c4, (Ac4). This to clear the row so that the king can be castled as soon as possible, and to control the d5 square, since many times the black plans to play d5, weakening our central pawn of e4. The bishop there acts as a guardian so that it doesn't happen. Black will not be able to make that plan and has to spend time thinking of something else. The resulting position will be as follows.

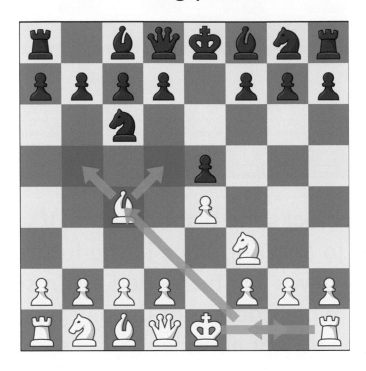

The next thing the opponent usually does is Nf6 to attack the e4 pawn, since they observe that there is no defender of that pawn, and it also develops their piece. While there are many moves that the opponent of black pieces can make, the move I just showed is played about 16,000 times more than the second most played, so I show you this variant because it is the one that you will find most likely in your games. The resulting position would be as follows.

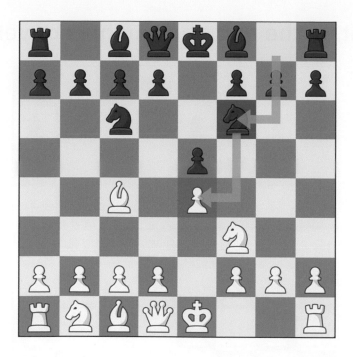

So the next move's objective will be somewhat obvious: defend the pawn. But this is where many people go wrong. The right move is d3, protecting the pawn with another pawn. Surely you are asking, "Why not defend with the knight, since it develops a piece?" The answer is that defending with the knight is not *really* defending, because of this trap that the black pieces have.

Assuming that, in the end, the knight is developed ...

... black would capture the pawn anyway. It is not defended because of a tactic ...

... since if you take back thinking that you won a knight ...

... they double attack you with the pawn, which would be protected by the queen.

At the end of the sideline, black would capture a piece, either the knight or the bishop (depending on which one you move) and will get rid of your pawns in the centre. Not only that, black will have their pieces control the centre. The one who controls the centre usually has an advantage from dominating more squares.

(final position after variant)

The correct move, in the previous position, is to protect not with the knight but with the pawn. That is, d3.

Then black can make two correct moves. In both cases, the response from white will be the same. They can do either h6 or bishop e7.

H6 is usually done because they are afraid of an attack called the *fried liver*, since you do not want the knight to jump to g5 and put a lot of pressure on the bishop in f7.

Although this can be defended, black has to know how to do it perfectly, so it is very difficult to stop the attack. That's why you can often come across h6 that controls the g5 square from knight jumps.

And you can also come across the Bc5 move, the idea of which is to get castled as quickly as possible, and on top of that, to develop a piece in an active place—one advantage of not having protected the pawn with the other pawn as we discussed before.

To any of these moves, your answer as a player of white pieces should be as follows:

You play c3, with two main ideas. First, if at any time you wanted to advance the queen pawn one step further, it would be protected three times by your pawn, knight, and queen; if it is advanced directly, it would only be protected by the knight and the queen.

Second, you play c3 to develop the queen and put immediate threats on black, since you would threaten many points in his position.

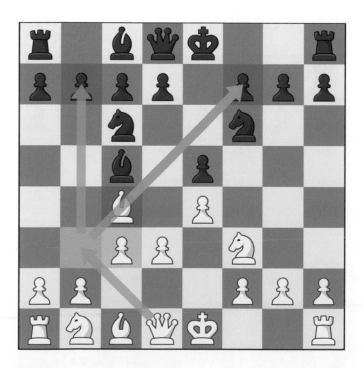

The most common response to c3 is to castle, since c3 is a move that is usually used to attack. That's why they castle, so that their king is safe from any danger.

Your answer will be to castle too. You are going to attack, you are going to take all the pieces to the attack, and you are going to leave the king without many pieces to defend himself, so putting your king under security is very important.

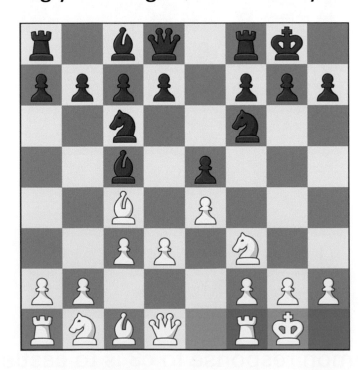

We have almost reached the end. What black usually does now is to think that the e5 pawn is defended, which is true, but only by a knight. If they want to move the knight, they will lose the pawn, so they usually play d6 to protect the pawn, to be able to move the knight in case an attack by white comes, and to not have to worry about the pawn.

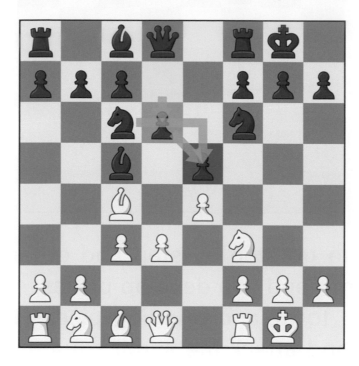

And with this, we have finished the Italian opening. With this opening, you will have many open lines to be able to take your pieces to the attack. The main thing to do after all of this depends on how you want to play the game.

Do you want to be very aggressive? I recommend you play bishop g5, pin their knight, and try to bring all the possible pieces to attack any of the three pawns that are red in the diagram.

Do you want to go step by step and organize the attack calmly? I recommend you develop pieces, such as playing knight from b1 to d2 and bringing pieces like the bishop to the attack, and attack the same squares as mentioned before (the red pawns).

For your dark-square bishop and your d2 knight to go on the attack, you first move the rook from f1 to e1 so that the knight then passes to f1 and the bishop can go out to g5. Then you take the knight to g3 to get in front of those pawns to attack (a plan carried out by many great masters).

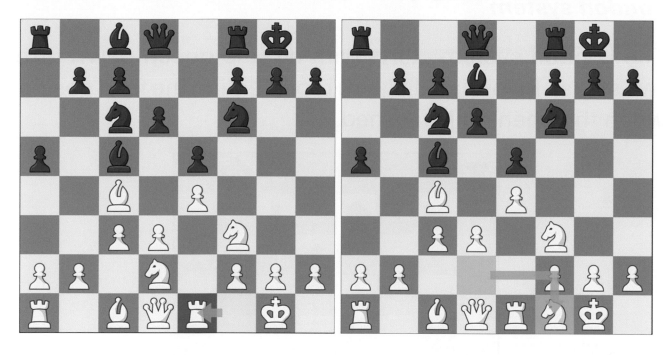

1st   2nd

3rd   4th

You have already seen the Italian opening. If you think it is not your type of play and that you will not like it, or you just want to see more openings and choose a better one for you, keep reading.

London system

The London system starts with d4 (the queen pawn takes two steps). Below is a diagram representing the final position when the opening is finished.

The purpose of this move is to dominate the central squares. They are the most important squares on the board, since almost all the action occurs through these squares.

Then black makes the d5 move, with the same purpose: control the central squares and prevent the white pawn from advancing further and taking more squares from the opponent—in this case, the black pieces.

The next thing that white will do is develop the knight that is in g1 to f3. This movement is written as Nf3, and it has two purposes: to clear the way so that the king can castle as quickly as possible and be under security, and to bring more pieces to the game and become more active.

Once this move is made, the opponent will believe that they are playing a queen's gambit, a fashionable opening due to the TV series of the same name (joke), and will make the e6 move, which is typical in these structures and also protects the central pawn in prophylaxis.

The next thing you are going to play is bishop f4. You develop this bishop since, with the next series of manoeuvres, your bishop would be locked up if it stayed in c1.

And now, whatever black does (the images I'm going to show are the most-played moves), you are going to do a triangle with the pawns in e3 and c3 so that the pawn in d4 is very consolidated.

As you will see, this opening does not have many variants. You simply have to know this series of moves, since you will always make the same ones.

What black does next is get castled.

This is simply to put the king under security.

Then what you are going to do is develop the knight towards the centre, since as I told you before, it is better this way compared with developing it towards a3:

This move has a simple explanation. You are only developing a piece so that you become more active.

Black will develop their knight through d7 or c6. Both squares are good, but you are more likely to encounter Nd7. You are also going to develop with the bishop in e2, although the best option is bishop d3. Based on my experience, I recommend bishop e2 for beginners, since it is more comfortable to play and you also save yourself the complication of your knight being pinned. You prevent that beforehand and thus save yourself discomfort in the future.

The most common thing in terms of black moves is that they play b6. This is to develop their bishop through b7 and joining that diagonal:

And then you get castled, to put your king under safety

The next move of black will be bishop b7, developing through that diagonal, as we expected.

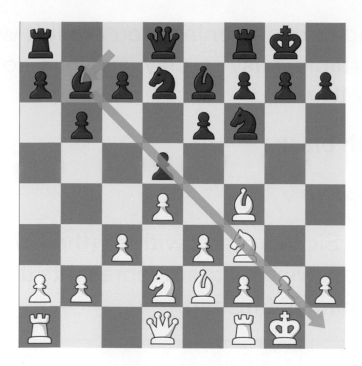

And as the last move of the opening, you are going to play h3. This to protect your bishop. Since the triangle we made before blocks the escaping route of the bishop, a common plan of black is to make h6 and g5, trapping it. With h3, we prevent that.

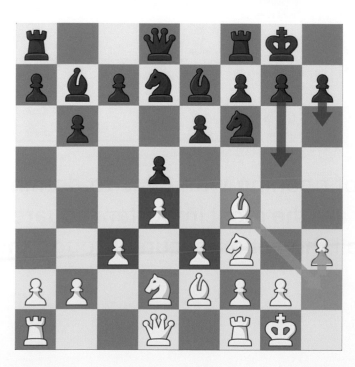

And at the end of this opening, you are left with a position that is comfortable, easy to play, and has no weaknesses. You are ready to win.

Openings with black

Hedgehog Sicilian

The Hedgehog Sicilian starts with e4 (the king's pawn takes 2 steps). The following diagram represents the final position when the opening is finished.

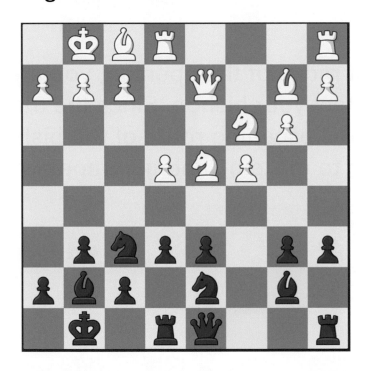

The purpose of opening with e4 is to dominate the central squares. They are the most important squares on the board, since almost all the action occurs through those squares:

What we are going to do now is what is called the Sicilian opening/defence. It consists of fighting for the centre but not with the central pawns, as you will have controlled the d4 square so that the white pieces cannot play d4, gaining space.

Next, white plays a very usual move, such as knight f3 (Nf3).

And what you will do next is simply prepare the future advance of the d pawn towards d5 to destabilize their centre, and you end up gaining space, leaving them with notorious weaknesses.

You will achieve this with the e6 move, as it protects the d5 square. On top of that, it opens the way for the development of the bishop.

White thinks, *Black wants to win control over the centre, and I can't allow that.* So what they will do is advance the pawn to d4 even if after the capture, the knight is in a somewhat strange position so that black does not have such a solid centre.

That position transforms into this one after those exchanges of central pawns.

What you're going to play now is a6.

This with a deep idea, in the Sicilian, that black wants to get to make the d5 play in good conditions.

However, they cannot, because white has a move that bothers black a lot—that is, bishop b5.

This delays the development of all black pieces, and it doesn't allow the pawn to move, as it is pinned. A6 avoids that idea, since white can no longer put any piece in b5; otherwise, they'll lose material.

The following moves are simple. The only thing that white does is develop its bishop to get castled as soon as possible, and so does black when moving its knight.

What white does is what we previously discussed: get castled.

Black plays d6, which seems like a strange move since what we wanted to do from the beginning was d5. However, if you do, you will be making a serious mistake. If you do that, white will happily take the pawn on d5, and when you recapture, white will have the column to come and attack your king with the rook (not a very pleasant situation).

Instead of the pawn of the d column being the advanced one, it should be the one on the e column, since there is no pawn that can capture it. This way, no columns will open through which your opponent could attack you. So, the e pawn should be the advanced one.

And also, now white square bishop can be developed (by d7). So doing d6 is a smart move.

Now, white plays c4, since they know that e5 is going to come at some point and they can't avoid it. What white does is take a space but on the right side; since they can't control the centre, they try to control other squares.

And now black plays g6, for two reasons: first, playing d6 makes the black-squared bishop more restricted, making the diagonal of h8 to a1 a better place for it; and second, to get castled as soon as possible.

After a few basic moves, where white does the same but with their bishop on c3 and black gets to castle …

... knights of both white and black develop.

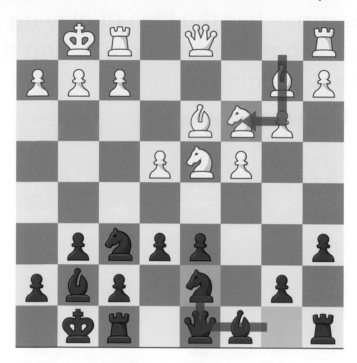

Both white and black develop their rooks, placing them at the e column in case it opens so that they become more active.

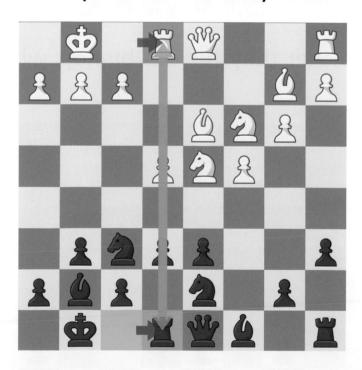

And here comes a strange move played by all the players of white pieces who have reached this depth in the opening: bishop f1. White realizes that the bishop is not very useful in d3 and prefers to manoeuvre it to a better place. It goes to f1, since this move has the idea of playing g3 so that the bishop has the diagonal open (on g2), and that the king is safer as it has a defending piece.

Black observes that they have a bishop who is not doing much ...

… and they want to develop it, so they play b6 to get the bishop out to b7, in the big diagonal.

Now white plays queen d2, which develops the queen to a slightly more active square and connects the rooks, and black moves bishop b7 as expected.

And we have finished learning the Hedgehog Sicilian. At the end of this sequence of moves, you are left with a rocky position that is difficult to penetrate due to how active your pieces are. It also has some weaknesses, mainly pawns, but that does not have a complex solution. Other than that, you will have a position that is usually very advantageous and comfortable to play.

We are almost done learning all the openings. Continue reading!

Slav defence

The Slav defence starts with d4 (the queen pawn takes two steps). Below is a diagram representing the final position when the opening is finished.

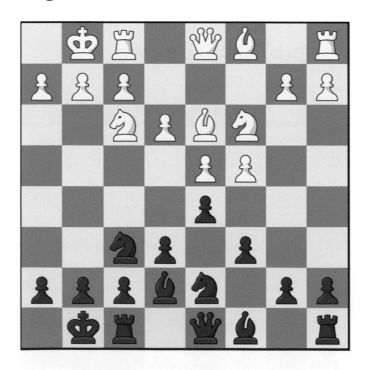

The purpose of beginning with d4 is to dominate the central squares. They are the most important squares on the board, since almost all action occurs through these squares.

Then symmetrical moves are made by both sides, to dominate the centre and to protect their central pawn, as you can see in this image.

Then white plays c4 to attack the centre, and does not mind being captured, because a central pawn is worth more than a lateral one, such as the pawn of c4. White would like to remove that pawn from the centre.

And black consolidates the centre by playing c6.

If you look closely, you'll see the same triangle as the London system.

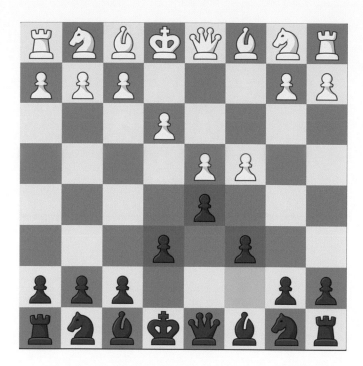

The good thing about this opening is that if you know the London system, you already know this opening, because it is exactly the London system only inverted, with black.

Continuing, both players take out and develop their knights.

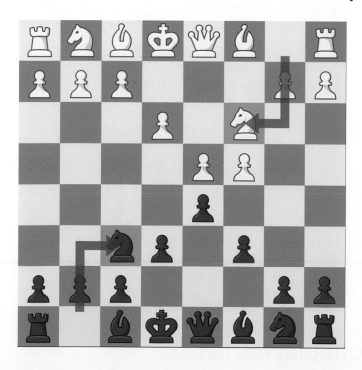

White takes out their bishop to develop it and get castled quickly, and black develops their knight to d7.

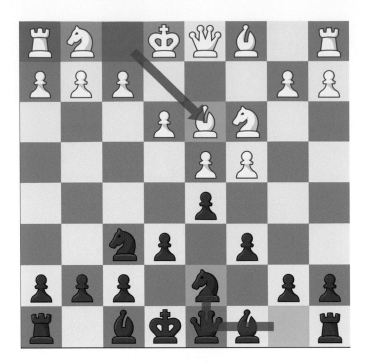

White now takes out their knight to castle and to become more active. Black does the same, developing their bishop to get castled as well.

And finally, both players castle.

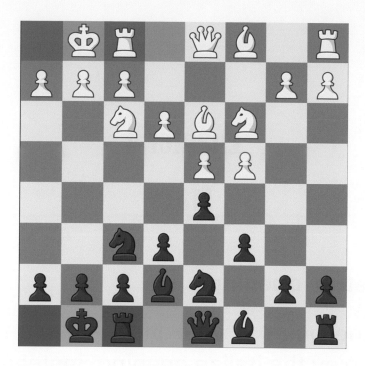

As you can see, this opening is very easy to play and has great similarity with the London system.

The good thing about both these openings with black is that they are very solid, they have no weaknesses, and even better, you can use them with almost any move that white makes. You can play them without issue. That is why I played them in tournaments: for their versatility and simplicity.

We have now finished seeing all the openings.

Chapter 4

Traps

Trap in the Petrov opening

Surely at some point in your life, you will encounter the Petrov. If you play the Italian opening, instead of protecting their pawn in the second move with the knight, black counterattacks and attacks your pawn as well, giving rise to this position.

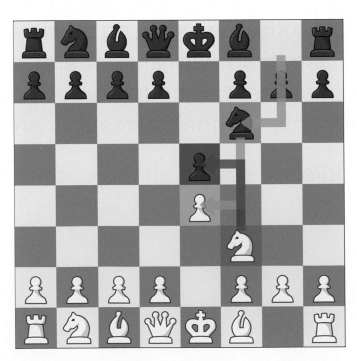

The right thing (if you are playing white) is to take black's pawn ...

… and see if they fall into the trap.

If they take back your pawn this way, the trap has begun:

What you have to do now is simply attack the knight with your queen, from e2, so that black is looking at the king, if all the pieces are removed from the column.

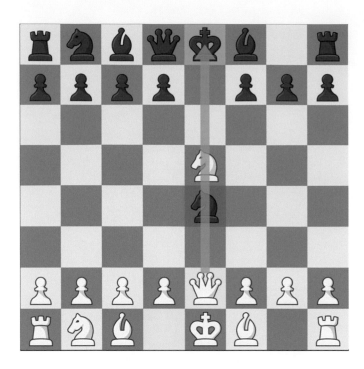

The most common thing in this position is that the knight goes back as if nothing had happened.

However, with the next move, you will make it clear that they have just lost the game.

Remember that we put the queen looking in X-ray at the king? We did it for this moment, since you are going to attack the rival's queen and at the same time give a check so that black can't simply move the queen out of danger, in the following way:

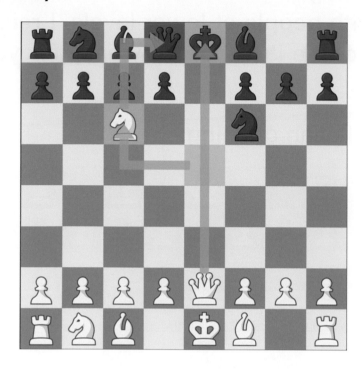

And now, whatever black does, you will get to take their queen, since if they cover themselves from the check with a knight or a bishop, you will take their queen with the knight, and you have an extra queen.

However, if they cover the check with the queen, you do the same. You take their queen with the knight, and you already have an extra queen. No matter what black does, they are completely lost.

And you're ready to win the game.

Shilling gambit

This is played by black, although I do not recommend it for tournaments or important events, because it is very easy for someone to beat you if they know how to neutralize it. Playing your position in that case will not be the most comfortable thing in the world. On the other hand, if you are playing with people at lower levels, I recommend that you use it, because it will be very easy for your opponent to fall into it.

They play the Italian opening.

You play knight d4.

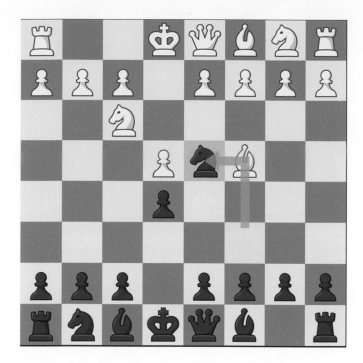

Here you will see if your rival is greedy. If they are, they will take the pawn immediately.

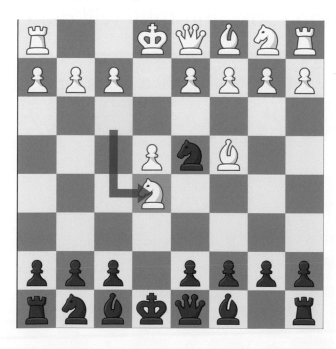

Now, with a lot of cold blood, you are going to play queen g5 and start a trap that your opponent will never forget.

At this point, white thinks that if they capture in f7 with the knight, they will most likely win the game, since they attack the queen and the rook, and they will gain material.

However, you have an ace up your sleeve, since you are going to make the move *queen takes g2* (Qxg2), attacking white's rook.

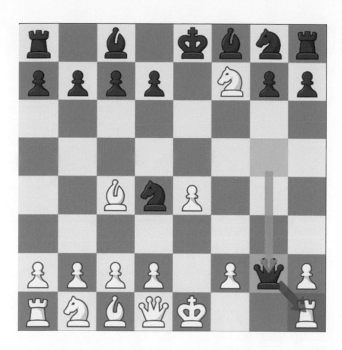

If white takes your rook, you take theirs, with check. When the sequence ends, their knight will end up getting lost, since they can't get it out of there. White tends to move the rook next to the king to protect it.

White's downfall has come, since you now have queen takes on e4. If they cover themselves from the check with the queen, you take it with the knight, and you are ready to win.

Many, to not lose the queen, will cover themselves with the bishop. But you will checkmate them with knight f3 (Nf3 checkmate).

And you just won the game.

Elephant trap

The elephant trap appears when a queen's gambit is played, and the next position appears where white pins a black knight, and black—instead of unpinning themselves with bishop e7—plays knight d7 with the simple purpose of not having doubled pawns in case the bishop is exchanged for the knight.

In this position, white thinks they are attacking the pawn two times while black only defends it once. (The knight does not count, since it is pinned, and if it moves, the queen is lost.)

And they end up taking on d5. Once everything is exchanged, the resulting position would be as shown.

However, white does not realize that they have just fallen into the elephant trap, since what black does now is take that knight without fear of losing the queen.

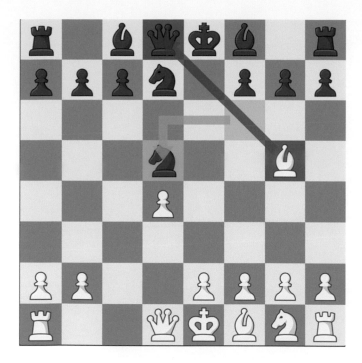

If white takes the queen, black has the bishop's move: bishop b4 check

That forces white to cover themselves from the check with the queen. The bishop captures the queen, the king recaptures the bishop, and then the black king takes the bishop of d8.

And at the end of the line, black has been left with an extra piece.

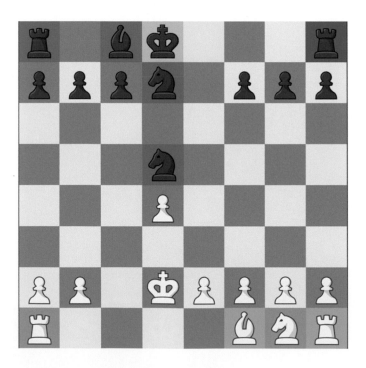

So black is ready to win the game.

Rubinstein trap

This is given with the following position derived from the queen's gambit.

In this position, black plays knight e4 to cover the so-dangerous diagonal that the bishop and queen are using to attack.

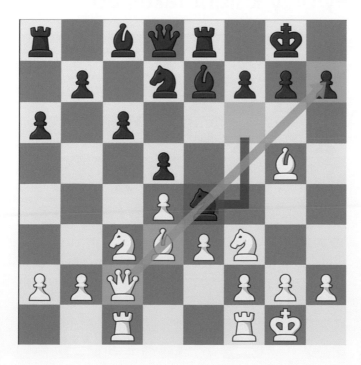

White moves the bishop from g5 to f4. When black moves the knight, the bishop on g5 is attacked, and then black plays f5 so as not to lose a pawn when all the pieces are exchanged in e4.

However, now white has a move that wins at least one pawn, since they play knight takes d5.

The best move for black is to ignore that they have lost a pawn and continue the game. However, what if we take this knight?

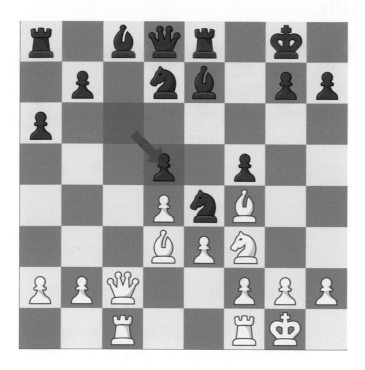

Well, now we lose the queen because of the next move: bishop c7 trapping the black queen.

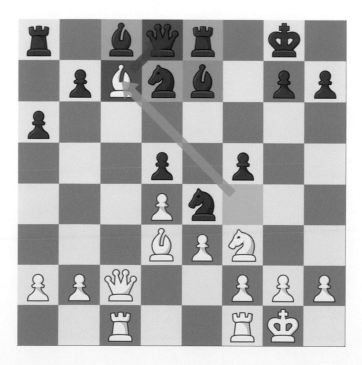

So white ends up winning the queen and therefore the game.

Fajarowicz trap

The following trap can only be played if black plays the Budapest gambit.

If you get into the mainline, the variant ends here.

Now is when white can be wrong. Many players who are solid play g3 to take the bishop to the long diagonal to be active.

However, they have just made a huge mistake. The trap starts with knight by f2! Incredible sacrifice.

That forces white to do something, otherwise either the queen or the rook will fall, and 100 per cent of the players who have had this position have played king takes knight.

However, now black has bishop takes g3 check, giving a discovered attack, attacking white's queen with theirs.

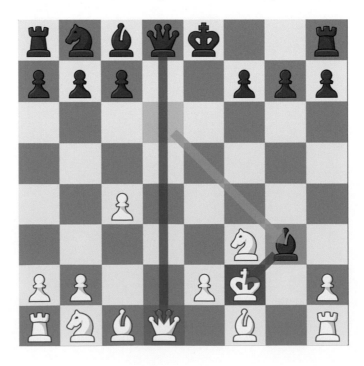

And now whatever white does, the queen will fall, whether it takes the bishop or not, since it cannot defend the queen.

And at the end of the whole variant, black has an extra queen and can already win the game.

Chapter 5
Endgame

The endgame technique that I consider the most important for every chess beginner is called the *magic square* or the *square rule*.

This is used when there are only kings and pawns. It is used to calculate if a king gets to catch a pawn before it promotes.

Take this position.

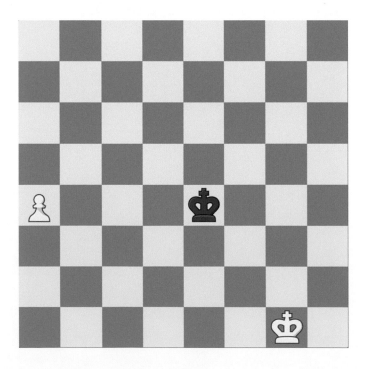

You are playing black. It is white's turn, and they advance their pawn. The question is, does your king get to stop the pawn, or does the pawn reach the end? Instead of counting step by step—if the king arrives or does not arrive—make a mental square with a side length that's the number of squares between the pawn and the promoting square. In this case, there are four squares.

You are left with this square.

As long as the king is inside the mentally drawn square, the king will reach to stop the pawn. If the king is out of the square, the king will not be able to stop the pawn.

As in the following position.

In this position, the king is not inside the square, so the king is not going to be able to stop the pawn.

This trick will be especially useful in faster time-formatted games because you save a huge amount of time not calculating all the steps of the pawns and your king individually.

Chapter 6

Vocabulary

Before your introduction to the world of chess begins, you must first know a series of words that are used to express concepts.

absolute pin: This occurs when a piece attacks an enemy piece, but it cannot move, because otherwise, that piece would attack the king.

activity: Refers to how many squares a piece controls. For example, if a rook is active, it controls a large number of boxes in its column and rows.

aggressive: An aggressive game mode forces your opponent to make plays that do not interest them. An aggressive player gains space and does not stop creating threats.

backward pawn: Backward pawns are those that are weak and not protected by any other pawn, which makes them a liability.

bishop pair: Term that is associated with having both bishops—the one with white squares and the one with black ones. That is a small advantage for those who own it, since in the endgame, when there are fewer pieces, the position is open and bishops can get from one side to another as quickly as possible—unlike knights, which would need several moves.

capture en passant: A special move that occurs when the rival moves one of his pawns two squares ahead, and right next to some pawn of yours. In this case, when capturing en passant, the pawn that performs the move stays in the position, as if the pawn that moved had moved only one step. This move can only occur at the precise moment when the opponent makes the move. It cannot be made several moves after.

castling: Chess move in which the king moves two steps towards the direction in which it wants to be castled, and the rook puts itself next to the king. This move is used so that the king is not in the centre, where it is most vulnerable, but on one side of the board.

check: Move that threatens the king of the rival with one of your pieces.

checkmate: Action that results at the end of the game, with the victory going to the one who performs it. This occurs when the king of the rival is in check but cannot move anywhere without being threatened or covered with any other piece.

closed position: A position in which both players lack much mobility, which usually occurs when there are a series of pawns that get in the way and block the position.

compensation: A compensation means you have less material, but your pieces are very active, such that the material disadvantage is almost none or is not noticed.

counterplay: Activity that the pieces acquire in compensation for a weak position. It is used when neutralizing your opponent's attack while you counterattack.

deflection: A tactic where the one who performs it deflects, as the name itself indicates, a rival's piece that was performing an important task, such as controlling a square or defending a piece.

development: In chess, development refers to pieces (not counting pawns) being taken out to play. In other words, they do not stay in the front row but take action.

double attack: A move that performs an attack on two different pieces at the same time.

doubled/tripled pawns: *Doubled pawns* means that there are two pawns in the same column. If they are *tripled pawns*, there will be three pawns in the same column. This disfavors the mobility of these pieces, so having them is a disadvantage.

draw: Draw is called in those positions in which neither side can make progress. The result is half a point for each.

endgame: Part of the game where there are fewer pieces and where the kings take on more activity.

exchange sacrifice: An exchange that disfavors (material-wise) one of the players but is done to achieve a greater and more important objective, such as killing the enemy king or increasing the activity of the pieces.

exchange: Action in which a piece is captured, and the rival captures back. This occurs when both pieces are of the same value or the same material; otherwise, it is called *exchange sacrifice*.

gambit: Opening where one or more pawns are sacrificed to achieve an activity or development of the pieces superior to those of the rival.

material: The value of a piece; each piece has its value.

open position: A position in which there are many columns, rows, and diagonals through which both players can move their pieces with ease.

positional: Game mode in which a player makes the most of the turns and times lost by the opponent and the small inaccuracies to increase their advantage little by little.

relative pin: Same concept as the *absolute pin*, only that in this case, instead of being nailed by the king, it is for another piece.

sides: Sides of the board. In chess there are two: queenside and kingside. The queenside is the entire area from column *a* to column *d* (a and d included), and the kingside is the entire area from column *e* to column *h* (e and h included). So, it is the side of the board where these pieces are located.

simplification: Strategy that is used when one player has more material than the other and exchanges pieces so that the position is simplified—and there are fewer pieces, so the advantage is noticeable. Thus, that player wins more easily.

space: The number of squares a player occupies or controls.

stalemate: A position very similar to checkmate, in which the player who has to move cannot move any of their pieces and not even their king, but they are not being checked (that is the difference between *checkmate* and *stalemate*). If this happens, the result of the game will be a draw.

tempo: A single movement performed. When a player achieves the expected result in fewer moves than expected, they are considered to have won a tempo, and if it takes longer than expected, a tempo is lost.

About the Author

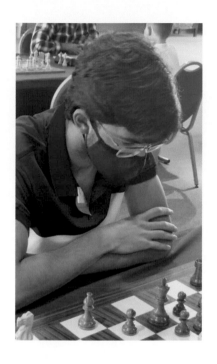

Aryan Jain Ascanio is a Spanish chess player and former Canary Islands mental calculation champion who, at age sixteen, won against a chess grandmaster. He has been competing in chess tournaments since age ten, and is working toward his official ELO qualification. Today, Aryan is studying to be an aerospace engineer.

Printed in the United States
by Baker & Taylor Publisher Services

Printed in the United States
by Baker & Taylor Publisher Services